Genre Biography

Essential Question
How do people meet personal challenges?

AGAINST THE ODDS

BY KIM GRISWELL

CHAPTER 1
A WAY TO PLAY

Jim Abbott was born in 1967 in Michigan. Growing up, he wanted to play baseball. But Jim was born without a right hand. The other kids in his neighborhood didn't let him join their games.

Jim's parents knew he had to be brave to live up to his **potential**. They told him to go back to the other kids and tell them he wanted to play. This time, he joined the game.

Jim had to learn how to play baseball with one hand. He learned to throw and catch with his left hand. This **compensated** for not having a right hand. His dad helped him figure out and **develop** a special way to pitch. They called it the "glove-hand switch."

Many children enjoy playing Little League baseball.

Jim also learned to bat with one hand. He held the bat with his left hand and balanced the handle on his right arm. The most important thing Jim learned was to focus on what he had, rather than on what he did not have.

When Jim was 11, he played on the Little League **pitcher's mound**. He pitched so well that no one on the other team hit the ball. This was his first no-hitter.

THE GLOVE-HAND SWITCH

Fans loved to watch Jim Abbott's glove-hand switch. These are the moves:

1. Abbott throws the baseball with his left hand. He keeps a fielder's glove balanced on the end of his right arm.
2. When he throws the ball, he quickly switches the glove onto his left hand.
3. After he catches the ball, Abbott holds the glove using his bent right arm. He pulls his left hand out of the glove.
4. He takes the ball out of the glove with his left hand. He gets ready to throw again.

When he entered junior high school, Jim could throw a ball at 80 miles per hour. In high school, he quickly got a spot on the varsity team.

Both the catcher and the pitcher need to be ready to field a bunt.

Coaches of other teams tried to find a flaw, or weakness, in Jim's pitching. Some thought Abbott's glove-hand switch would make it hard for him to field a **bunt**. A bunt is when a ball is hit short. Often the pitcher has to field these hits. Abbott might not get to the ball in time. One coach decided to **implement** a plan, or **strategy**. He told eight batters to bunt Abbott's pitches. Jim retired, or struck out, seven of the eight batters.

Jim Abbott became a great batter, too. He hit seven home runs during his senior year. His team lost only three games.

STOP AND CHECK

What helped Abbott play baseball so well?

CHAPTER 2

AGAINST THE ODDS

Jim Abbott had a fantastic baseball season in his last year of high school. A professional team, the Toronto Blue Jays, wanted him to join them. Abbott had to decide. He could play for a professional team right after high school. Or he could wait until he'd finished college.

The University of Michigan offered Abbott a full scholarship. Then the Blue Jays offered him a $50,000 bonus. Abbott had to carefully consider, or **assess**, his options. He chose to go to college.

Students walk on the University of Michigan campus.

During Abbott's first year of college, the media became interested in him. But they paid attention because he didn't have a right hand. Abbott thought having no right hand was **peripheral** to his success. It was his hard work that mattered.

In his second year of college, Abbott joined the United States national baseball team. This was an **amateur**, or nonprofessional, team. He helped the team win a silver medal in the Pan American games. He did not give up a single **earned run** in that competition.

At the end of that year, Abbott was chosen as the first baseball player to win the Sullivan Award.

THE SULLIVAN AWARD

The Amateur Athletic Union's Sullivan Award is the top amateur sports award. It is given to the most outstanding amateur athlete in the United States for that year. The winner is chosen for athletic ability. The winner must also show leadership, good character, and sportsmanship.

To Abbott, it seemed as if millions of people took pictures when he practiced in Japan.

In his junior year of college, reporters often asked Abbott his least favorite question: "How do you play baseball with just one hand?"

"I don't even think about it," he told them. "Then you guys come around to remind me."

Abbott continued to win games. This winning **streak** gave him confidence. Then he earned a spot on the United States Olympic baseball team in 1988. Abbott, with Team USA, went on a world tour. The tour ended at the Olympics in Seoul, South Korea.

The best part of Abbott's summer was the **series** against Japan's national team. The Japanese were fascinated by Abbott's one-handed playing. He became a hero in Japan.

By the time they reached Seoul, Abbott had become the team's top starting pitcher. Coach Mark Marquess did not let him pitch for the early games. He wanted to save his best pitcher for the final game.

The final game was against Japan. Abbott started strong, but in the sixth inning, his pitching **deteriorated**. Coach Marquess had to decide whether to keep Abbott in the game.

The coach thought Abbott could still turn the game around. He was right. The United States won its first gold medal in baseball.

STOP AND CHECK

What were Abbott's successes during his college years?

Abbott pitched the United States team to an Olympic win.

CHAPTER 3

INTO THE MAJORS

After the Olympics, Abbott was ready to join a professional baseball team. The California Angels had chosen him to play for them.

Crowds of reporters and fans came to watch Abbott at **spring training** in 1989. The game had to be moved from the practice field to the regular stadium. Abbott pitched for three innings and struck out four batters.

Abbott bats for the California Angels.

Many reporters asked Abbott how he could pitch so well with just one hand. He replied, "I've been doing this since I was five years old. It's as natural as tying my shoes."

Abbott made the California Angels' A team. Only 15 players had ever gone straight to the major leagues. Usually, players practice in the minor leagues first.

Angels fans loved Abbott from the beginning. The first time he stepped onto the pitcher's mound, the crowd stood up and cheered. The Angels didn't win that game, but the fans didn't **desert** Abbott. They stuck with him. They gave him a second standing **ovation**, cheering for him again at the end of the game.

The day that Abbott made the A team was one of the happiest days in his life.

Losing his first game in the major leagues worried Abbott. He knew he had to work harder to succeed.

Abbott pitches for the California Angels.

Abbott's hard work paid off. He pitched 12 winning games that season. No other major league pitcher in his first season had played that well since 1924.

Abbott had a great record by the end of the 1991 season. He had an 18–11 win-loss record. He became the highest-paid fourth-year pitcher in baseball history.

In December 1992, the Angels traded Abbott to the New York Yankees. It could have been a **devastating** experience, but Abbott refused to give up.

STOP AND CHECK

Why did Abbott do so well with the Angels?

CHAPTER 4

THE PUBLIC STAGE

In New York, Abbott pitched a game that no one has forgotten. The Yankees were playing against the Cleveland Indians, and Abbott was pitching. After the first three innings, the Yankees were winning 3–0. By the sixth inning, the Indians still didn't have any runs.

The crowd stood up for every pitch in the last two innings. Abbott remained calm. By the end of the game, he had pitched a no-hitter. No other Yankee pitcher had done that in 10 years.

Yankee team members congratulate Abbott.

Abbott pitched for the White Sox in 1995.

Abbott had reached the **summit** of his career. He was one of baseball's best pitchers. This made the media pay more attention to him. The attention started to affect his pitching. He was not pitching as well as usual.

In addition, the Yankees' owner said Abbott wasn't focusing on baseball enough. Abbott tried to meet a disabled child each time he traveled with the team. The owner blamed this **charity** work for Abbott's poor pitching.

The Yankees didn't sign Abbott for the next season, so Abbott joined the Chicago White Sox. Then in 1996, he played for the Angels again. But his pitching was not as strong as it used to be.

The next spring, the Angels cut Abbott from the team. Abbott was disappointed, but he didn't stop trying. He worked his way back to the major leagues for two more seasons.

Abbott retired from major league baseball in 1999. Now he encourages people to focus on what they *can* do. He inspires them to work hard and chase their dreams—just as he did.

JIM ABBOTT'S PITCHING STATISTICS

Year	Team	W	SO
1989	California Angels	12	115
1990	California Angels	10	105
1991	California Angels	18	158
1992	California Angels	7	130
1993	New York Yankees	11	95
1994	New York Yankees	9	90
1995	Chicago White Sox	6	45
1995	California Angels	5	41
1996	California Angels	2	58
1998	Chicago White Sox	5	14
1999	Milwaukee Brewers	2	37

W–Win: number of games where pitcher was pitching while his team took the lead and went on to win.

SO–Strikeout: occurs when a batter receives three strikes during his time at bat. Pitchers want to throw as many strikeouts as possible.

STOP AND CHECK

How did the media affect Jim Abbott's pitching?

Respond to Reading

Summarize

Use important details from *Against the Odds* to summarize the selection. Your graphic organizer may help you.

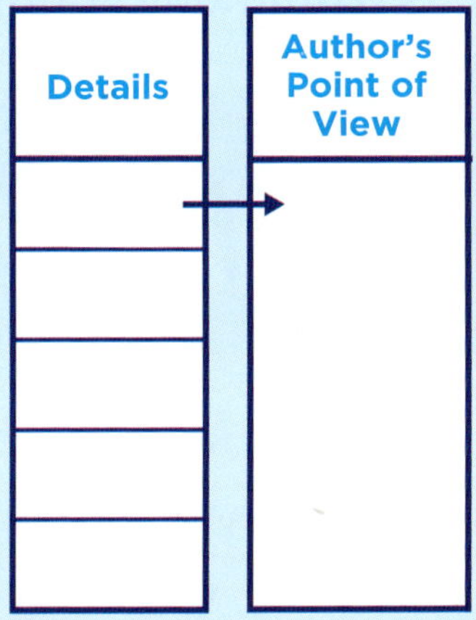

Text Evidence

1. What is the author's point of view toward Jim Abbott? What clues show this? **AUTHOR'S POINT OF VIEW**
2. Find the word *flaw* on page 4. What clues help you to figure out the word's meaning? **VOCABULARY**
3. The author included two quotations. How do the quotations show what the author thinks about Abbott? Write about it. **WRITE ABOUT READING**

Genre Expository Text

Compare Texts

Read about a glove for people with communication challenges.

Talk with the Glove

José Hernandez-Rebollar (*air-NAHN-dehz ray-BOH-yar*) knew he wanted to be an electrical engineer. Electrical engineers design devices such as cell phones and robots.

In 1998, Hernandez-Rebollar came to the United States from Mexico. He had gotten a Fulbright Scholarship to study at a university in Washington, D.C.

Hernandez-Rebollar liked helping others meet challenges, and he liked inventing new devices. He wanted to figure out how to translate sign language into sound. "I want to produce something that deaf people can use in everyday life," he said.

The Acceleglove sends information to a computer that translates sign language into sound.

Language Without Sound

Hundreds of thousands of deaf people in the United States use American Sign Language (ASL). Friends, relatives, and others who talk to deaf people also use ASL.

Hernandez-Rebollar invented the Acceleglove. This glove helps deaf people to communicate with people who do not know ASL. In an emergency, the Acceleglove could save lives.

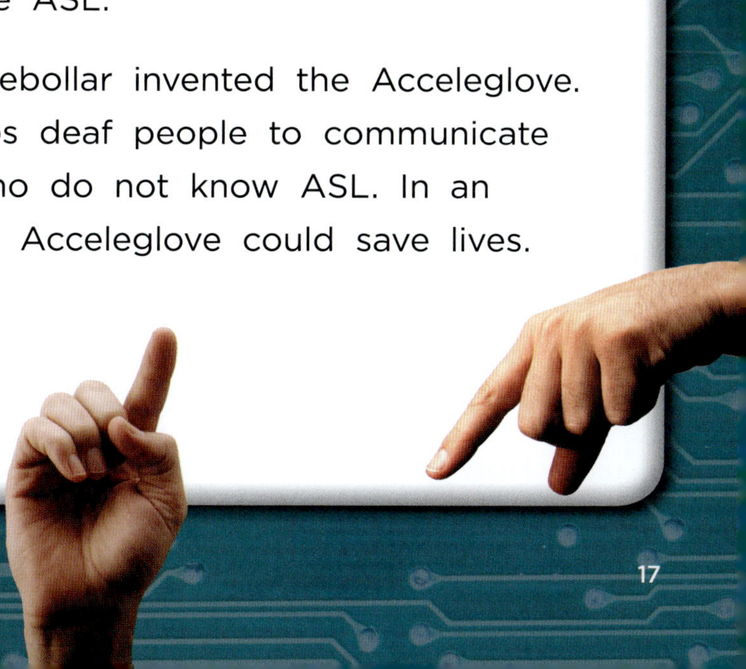

A Talking Glove

The Acceleglove is a glove with **sensors** on it. When you wear the glove, the sensors measure how you move your arm and hand. Electronics inside the glove send this information to a computer that changes the information into words. People can hear these words or read them on a computer screen.

Engineers are thinking of more ways to use the Acceleglove. Some possibilities are graphic design, robotics, and video gaming.

INVENT SOMETHING!

Step 1: Identify a problem.
Step 2: Brainstorm solutions.
Step 3: Choose a solution.
Step 4: Research the solution.
Step 5: Make a detailed plan.
Step 6: Design and build a model.
Step 7: Test the model.

Make Connections

Why did José Hernandez-Rebollar invent the Acceleglove? **ESSENTIAL QUESTION**

How are Jim Abbott and José Hernandez-Rebollar similar? **TEXT TO TEXT**

Glossary

bunt *(buhnt)* in baseball, to tap the ball lightly into the infield, without swinging the bat ***(page 4)***

earned run *(URNd run)* in baseball, a run scored not due to an error on the part of the fielding team ***(page 6)***

pitcher's mound *(PI-chuhrs mownd)* the raised circle of dirt in the middle of the infield on which a baseball pitcher stands ***(page 3)***

sensors *(SEN-suhrz)* devices that detect and measure something ***(page 18)***

series *(SEER-eez)* a set of games (usually three, during a regular baseball season) played between two teams over a few days ***(page 7)***

spring training *(spring TRAY-ning)* baseball practices and games held before the regular season starts ***(page 9)***

Index

Focus on Science

Purpose To explore how exercise affects your pulse

Procedure

Step 1 Work with a partner. Choose an exercise, such as skipping or jumping jacks. Set a goal, such as 100 jumping jacks.

Step 2 Ask your partner to take your pulse. He or she needs to check how many times your heart beats in one minute.

Step 3 Now start your exercise. Stop when you begin to feel out of breath. Ask your partner to check your pulse again. Then your partner takes a turn.

Step 4 After a rest, do your exercise again a few times. Try to get closer to your goal each time. Check your pulse each time.

Conclusion What do you notice as you get closer to your goal? How do you feel?